COMMERCIALS FROM A

JUNKYARD

TEXTS AND PHOTOGRAPHS BY GEORGE UTECH

Published by George W. Utech, 80 Harper Drive,
Pittsford, New York 14534

Designed and supervised by Robert L. Whiting,
of Bob Wright Studio, Inc.
Rochester, New York 14620

Printed by Harney Printing Corporation,
Rochester, New York 14625

Printed in the United States of America

To Krestie, Anna, Jenny, Dan and Jon Eric

3

Colossal rubbish!
Here, high-piled has beens
Rear a ragged pyramid.
These rejects rise,
A jagged monument.
This Pharaonic shape
Aspires to scrape the skies.
Burned out utility
Crowds on one spent heap.
A million miles expired
Mound this sheer, metallic tumulus.
Who, what, why? lies buried here,
Attended by untold millions of atoms.

Grazing green fields,
Munching lush grass,
They might have been sheep
Quietly growing wool and lean lamb chops.
Seeing them there like that,
Spread out on the pasture,
A docile English landscape came alive
Echoing "sheep may safely graze"
Courtesy of John Sebastian Bach.
Except, as we grew close,
They stood too still,
Flocked tin shells
Unbleating in the morning sun.
No wool. No meat.
Nor Turner. Nor J. S. Bach.
Hills rose 'round them,
Old mountains, worn down,
Cynical of such scenes,
That in their view will scarcely leave a scar.
We look again, but they remain,
Hard corpses, glinting in the sun.

Here, in the secret dark,
Eons of retrospective sun
Resurrected, booming,
Fuelling a holocaust.
Restrained through this iron-willed space,
It drove man and metal on.
How you pranced, you steed!
How you danced on fiery feet!
Now, all fires out, you sleep
While rust weighs on you like grief.

Still speed me on, Olympian spark!
Flash me, away and away.
Hurl my flesh, my mind,
On errands so numerous.
Grant my clay legs dynamic boots
To stride, a giant, over countryside.
We shall startle the dawn as we pass,
Laying concussions on the morning air.
Move me, glad-wheeled, on a glory ride.
Fling me, highgeared, at space.
Grant my going wings.

ow fetching, your brightwork,
Sheet metal sculpted so curvaceously.
How mighty your engine!
Most glorious your gearbox!
How your wheels circumflex!
All your glass and steel grace
Shine forth to stun the eye
While you exude such youth and promises.
You shall have names enscribed in chromium.
Your style shall be etched on every brain.
You shall be celebrated far and wide,
At the beginning and the end,
As the antecedent and apocalypse,
And all else in between.

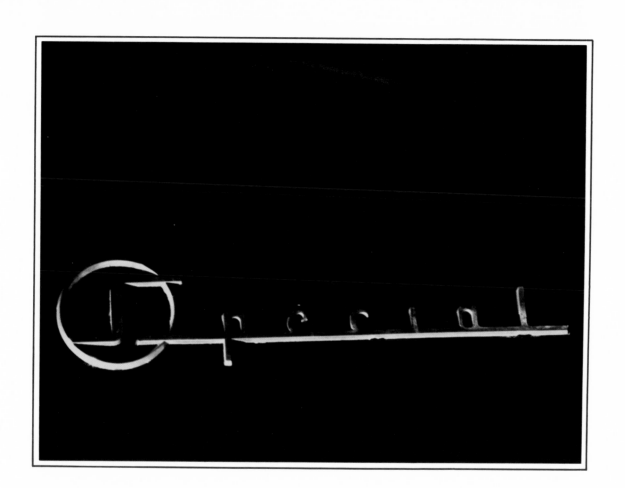

Fantastic, Capri!
You played, fanciful, free.
You gave quite a thrill
When you rode as a whim in the wind.
No one cared you were named
In honor of an island.

Wheels stilled,
Mobility cut off.
Call the roll:
Cadillac, Chevrolet,
Lincoln, Ford,
Dodge, Chrysler,
Rambler and the rest.
All races run. Errands at an end.
Gross space squeezed out,
What remains, remains beyond repair.
Crushed to a sullen rectangle.
Far from the showroom.
Swansong of the assembly line.
Carrion for the steel mill's mouth.
New shapes will rise from these,
Sent forth shining as these were,
Destined as these are.

Lightning swift,
Power swept these fibers as intelligence.
This vital center struck
A billion fires,
Sent tons of steel and flesh
Whistling on their way.
By means of these quick wits,
Blood and iron pressed
Toward a solid pact of speed.
Now torn out, disjoined, ripped off,
It cannot heal its hurt.
Without ceremony, the soft air
Smooths its cleverness.

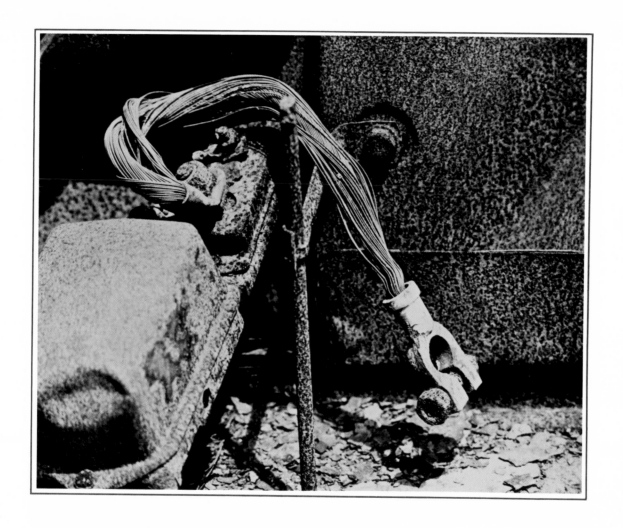

ere lies Atlas, in grim decease,
Inspiring epitaphs at great increase.
May I quote Mr. Webster, please?
Here lies *a giant*
Who was compelled to support
The heavens on his shoulders.
He was *in Homer*
A god in charge
Of the pillars of heaven.
Elsewhere *a king*
Changed into a mountain.

y thoughts run like a wheel
Whose center is not fixed.
From where have I come?
Where am I going?
Illusions spin in me:
I move, therefore I am.

20

A hundred thousand comings and goings
Collect here, in reminder.
Each turn of the handle, release of door,
A ritual of entrance and exit.
Possibilities, arrived, departed.
Beginnings and endings, memorialized.
Big tasks, little ones,
Shopping trips and rendezvous
Slow drives in the country
Trips to the zoo,
Children spilling out like waterfalls.
To and from work.
Doors closing on funerals,
Opening for mothers ready to give birth.
Slamming on crime,
On arguments and tender love,
On rich and poor alike;
Each here and there part
Of the grand entrance and exit.

Not likely a row of skulls,
But possibly shinbones.
How much they look like
Ossicles sunning themselves.
O talus! O tarsus! Do you know
How terribly temporal you are?

What if, somewhere in this pile of parietals,
As they scale and rust and rot,
A superior maxillary
Schemes and plans and plots.
What if, in your wildest wishbone dreams,
This whole valley of bones
Could be Ezekielized and come alive again?
Would you wish to rise,
Spine and sternum set aright,
Responsive and sesamoid,
Your cranium joined, and scaphoid?
Would you resume, if you could,
The tissues of steel, the heart of fire,
Body done up in plastic, fabric and whim,
To be joined to your four round whirlers again?

25

Spring, sprang, sprung
Push up, press down
Again, again, again.
God knows how many times.
Tire of thinking *how many*
As when we calculate heartbeats
Per hour, per day, per week, per year.
Balk at our complexity
And the quantities we could be divided into.
Why marvel?
Let these wonders rot.
Feel tired, here in the junkyard
Late in the afternoon.

t could be a graph,
Peaked at the end of whatever progress.
Some program, perhaps, with all ups and no downs?
It could be metal sculpture,
Mechanical intent gone astray,
Dreams dreamed from scrap.
It could be tendrils
Curling green, lively, ambitious,
About to scale a neat brick wall.
This, too, will dissolve, in time
Leaving a graceful line, to remember:
Iron aspiring toward some star.

Standing like bookends,
This impasse deadends.
Some madness drives them on, and on,
If only in one's mind
They push against another.
They point,
As if toward magnetic north,
As if from all ends of the earth.
Out of this mess,
A cry may come.
Let it be heard.
Let it be heard.

elmets and shields and armor
Knights long ago might have donned
For battle, with honor, to glory,
Such proud protection.
Such vain insignia exalt no more.
Forlornly, they stack
As in a museum.

32

A hundred pipers starting
Up a spring green glen
Move across blackened freeways
Sounding choruses of din.
Through little towns and great big cities
They beat our bodies numb,
Through window panes and stout brick walls
They pound on ear drum,
Split nerve ends, and raise
Clouds of chaos in the brain.
A thousand, thousand players
Thoroughly gone mad,
Blowing loud disharmony.
How long, my God, how long?

umpty Dumpty sat on the freeway
Trying to think through a new way.
All the trucks, cars and buses
Ran over Humpty and made him Dumpty.

36

Three-quarters fossil,
So severed from its former use
It might have been
A giant snail's abandoned house.
Imagine her
Crawling in the same, patient way
Almost since time began,
Her entire burden on her back,
Her purpose, her tedious path.
Earth aged while she passed
And ages wherever she has gone.

Better than crawling in slime
Just up from some primordial pond,
Better than stone ax and damp cave.
Tadpoles, swimming as usual
Can't know what we do:
Nothing's so much fun
As having evolved to drive the car.
Everyman, a kind of king!
His car, his kingdom.
He rules the steering wheel
As if by divine right.
O, yes, give it gas, give it gas.
Here's to our age come of age,
Here's to automotive might!
Three big cheers for cars, cars, cars!
Long live autocentricity!

alf up, half down,
It flip-flops in the wind.
Like praying hands
It forms a supplication
For quick return of carefree days
Gone by, for benedictory skies,
To be delivered from
The rain and air and sun
Which rip and beat upon.
No sparrow would ever nest
Within these scarecrow limbs.
No marrow warms these bones.

Your fractured sight
No longer clarifies the night.
Eyes out, robbed of light,
No more will you go, bright
On the far horizon
Hibeaming on and on,
A sudden wedge of light
Splitting through the night,
A small width of sight
Blazing red, red in aftermath.
Nearsighted, farsighted,
What does it matter now?
No more pedestrians to stare down,
No more angry looks
At chance stray dogs that cross your path.
No more surprising lovers in the park.
Gone, exotic eyefulls of spring landscape,
Fall colors will brighten and fade, unseen,
While all things large and small:
Playgrounds of children,
Parades, towers of buildings, and slums,
Flocks of birds, masses of people, crowds of cars;
None of it seen, none.
Brood, like Samson.

April air and soft rain
Bite at you, surprisingly voracious.
All out of doors will devour you.
You are on a slow schedule of ruin.
Time and atmosphere gnaw like vultures.
You erode and no one cares.
Atoms feast on you quietly.
The air grows thick above you
With your shape, released
In oxidizing flight.
Though human love and adoration
Once enfolded you with tenderness,
Look now, how fickle
Man's love for his machines.
You show a mortal wound.
Neglected, you perish,
As this smut rots you,
Spoiling you utterly until you disappear.
Change swarms around you like bees,
Pollinating your destruction.

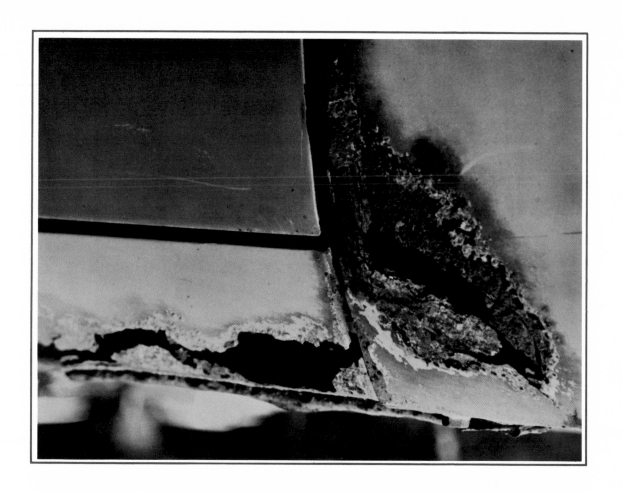

On Fleetwood, on Comet
On Cougar and Capri,
Now De Ville and Delta
Electra and Marquis:
To the top of the pile,
Over the junkyard wall,
Now rush away, rush away,
Rush away all.

The children of Detroit
Weep by many rivers.
Their grief stains
Flowing waters.
They rust through all seasons.
No words speak their sorrow.
Granted aspirations,
Iron ore might have chosen other ends.

She makes meat and milk
Among the ruins of a species
More recent than her kind.
The grass creeps to cover
Dark stains spreading
Where metal bleeds to death.

All gleaming arrogance,
He slithers through this shattered park,
A polished fiend,
Half beguiling, half terrifying.
How he glistens when he glides!
Hypnotic flim-flam, his shine
Suggests deceit, yet fixes
Fear in whom he meets, unblinkingly.
Wily reprobate,
His chromed style reminds
Of Janus, Judas, Brutus.

Put rudely into the back window,
The latticed, front end grill
Displays the doll quite delicately,
Perhaps to amend for all the harshness,
Perhaps to place neglect against violence
As kinder of the two.
What put the little figure there
Face down, forgotten in all her injuries,
Will remain a mystery.
Even if we care, we will never know.
If we knew, we might not care.
Whatever circumstance
Put front in back,
Tenderness and destruction in one scene,
Is gone, moved on, over, done.
Human presence has fled.
The doll gives no interviews.
A child's presence may be inferred.

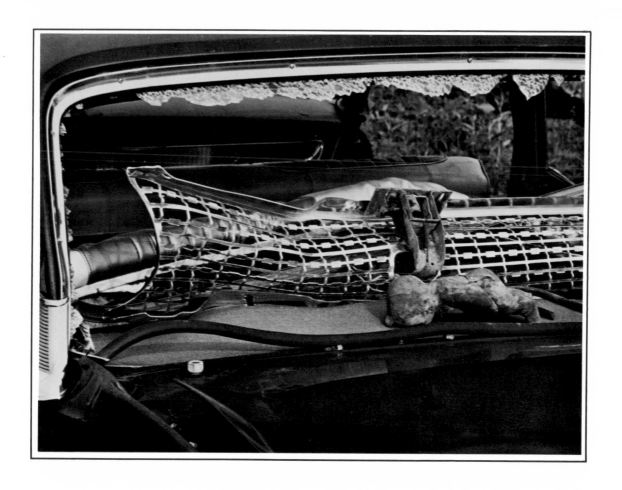

Fan belt ringed upon a foursquare,
Engine, at last, be still.
Your blades, fixed as cross,
No more revolve to kill
The air with savage edge,
The ear with brutal sound.

Cast from some moment's hand,
Glass shards heap
Jeweled by the swift, dark end.
The light radiates a rainbow
From that poor center, surprisingly.
They glow with possibilities.

ere, in the junkyard,
Black hours of brooding end.
Now morning strikes
A welder's torch above the ruins.
The junkyard, aha!
The jagged edges, slashes,
Rips, bashes, bumps;
All gashes and splinters,
Fractures, dents and lumps,
Barbs, shards and brokenness . . .
All, all are turning into something else.
Something else is at hand.

The photographs in this book were made in 1965 from negatives taken at various automobile junkyards and salvage depots. The texts were written in 1972. Neither the texts, nor the photographs, have been published previously.